PURPOSEFUL
VISION

PURPOSEFUL VISION

SEE YOUR VISION,
KNOW YOUR PURPOSE

LINTON BERGSEN

BALBOA.
PRESS

A DIVISION OF HAY HOUSE

Balboa Press books may be ordered through booksellers or by contacting:

Balboa Press
A Division of Hay House
1663 Liberty Drive
Bloomington, IN 47403
www.balboapress.com
1 (877) 407-4847

Because of the dynamic nature of the Internet, any web addresses or
links contained in this book may have changed since publication and
may no longer be valid. The views expressed in this work are solely those
of the author and do not necessarily reflect the views of the publisher,
and the publisher hereby disclaims any responsibility for them.

The author of this book does not dispense medical advice or prescribe the use
of any technique as a form of treatment for physical, emotional, or medical
problems without the advice of a physician, either directly or indirectly. The
intent of the author is only to offer information of a general nature to help you
in your quest for emotional and spiritual well-being. In the event you use any
of the information in this book for yourself, which is your constitutional right,
the author and the publisher assume no responsibility for your actions.

Certain stock imagery © Thinkstock.
Any people depicted in stock imagery provided by Thinkstock are models,
and such images are being used for illustrative purposes only.

ISBN: 978-1-4525-9387-6 (e)
ISBN: 978-1-4525-9386-9 (sc)
ISBN: 978-1-4525-9388-3 (hc)

Library of Congress Control Number: 2014904122

Printed in the United States of America.

Balboa Press rev. date: 3/31/2014

The true sign of intelligence is not knowledge but imagination

—ALBERT EINSTEIN

CONTENTS

INTRODUCTION

If seeing is believing, then every day you can be aware of your true purpose and passion in life. You have an imagination; therefore you have a vision.

You can literally see your future and how you want it to be—the dreams you want to pursue and the feelings they arouse within you—*when you are truly connected to your vision.*

Imagination is nothing more than visual images that allow you to see, in your mind's eye, everything inside of you that is wanting, waiting, and yearning to be set free.

When you take action based on faith and conviction toward your purpose, you can see and feel it in the very core of your being. You are driven to excel with confidence!

The freedom you feel comes from expressing yourself in the unique and profound way that you find welling up within you. This is what you were born to do!

You are constantly receiving inner guidance, feelings, and intuition about your possible future. It simply happens that way. If only you could harness and understand the true meaning, power, and source of all of these feelings that constantly want to propel you forward.

But you can! Pursue your true purpose in life by listening to the inner voice. It's there, and it's trying to guide you. Follow your hunches and your dreams.

Sometimes it may seem to you that you are walking through a maze, going nowhere in particular. You may feel exhausted and frustrated as a result of trying to understand the exact meaning of all the messages and promptings that are trying to lead you to your higher calling in life.

You know what you want. You want desperately to move from the ordinary to the extraordinary, from the mundane to the exciting, from boredom to exhilaration, in every area of your life.

But it's not happening quite as you planned.

There is a way to begin to unravel this ball of string, to undo any of the knots you find or have created.

In the pages that follow, you will find many tools that, when understood and applied, will begin to guide you toward unraveling your ball of string. Things will begin to make sense!

Use the same ball of string to wrap a present for yourself. Let your life be filled with gratitude and love for all that you are. Let your imagination and vision move you toward your dreams.

There is no limit to the supply of inspiration that is within you. It can always help and guide you through any situation in life. You'll find more knowledge, peace, and happiness than ever before.

It's time to follow and manifest your dreams!

CHAPTER 1

The *reality* of your vision will lead to the *realization* of your dreams!

You cannot create anything you want from life if you cannot see it as a possibility. Period. It's never going to happen.

In order for your dreams to manifest into reality, you must have a distinct vision to help you navigate through life. Having a vision is also critically important to substantiating the meaning of your life and validating the reason you are here.

Every single one of us has a vision. We may each call it by a different name—a *dream*, a *wish*, or a *hope*. But how do you get from having a dream to seeing it come true?

The long answer? Many things need to be set in motion and accomplished before your dream manifests itself.

The short answer? It begins with imagination.

THE IMPORTANCE OF IMAGINATION

Imagination is the only state of mind that allows us to be free from the limiting reality we live in. Allowing our imagination to flow freely liberates us from the restraints of regular life.

Imagination creates a vision for us to see what could be. Imagination gives us hope in the face of adversity because it has no limits. It allows us to believe in possibilities that would not otherwise exist. It allows us to feel invigorated, alive, optimistic, and enthusiastic. It connects us to a deeper part of ourselves.

I believe:

> *Imagination is the essence of sustained motivation toward the accomplishment of any goal.*

Imagination connects you continually and sustainably to a tangible outcome. It determines your behavior.

Did you realize that your imagination has an actual physiological impact on your emotions, allowing them to be evoked positively or negatively? When you imagine, you physically feel what *might* transpire if the situation you are imagining becomes a reality!

Let me give you an example. We have all had the experience of constantly imagining a negative outcome of an event and immediately feeling our hearts begin to race as anxiety rises up within us. Perhaps you were in a tense situation and wondered:

What will the medical test reveal?

Will I embarrass myself at this presentation? What if I forget what I'm going to say?

Are those police lights flashing behind me?

We've all been there—but entertaining negative thoughts produces the same stress and anxiety as if the potential outcome actually happened! The body is reacting with physical symptoms to the images provided by our minds.

The reverse effect can also be achieved. If we imagine a positive, uplifting experience, don't we feel excited, elated, and energized? What a difference!

The fact is, your body is simply hardwired to respond to your mind, and your mind responds to the pictures you feed it. It's the same for all of us.

Now here is where things get very interesting. Your emotions and behavior are also tied to the images you visualize. Though often underestimated, this is a very powerful combination.

Understand and internalize this truth: your imagination is a reference point. It will help you find your life purpose and future as you visualize it. It is all about the mental pictures you create.

Let me ask you something. How many times have you really had your imagination roam in the recesses of your mind to come up with a huge idea, and been spurred to move forward on that incredible idea, only to be told by others that it is impossible?

Don't they ask you why you would even think or imagine such a thing? And if you don't have the education, finances, or resources, they really give you grief! Regardless of their intentions, they try to ground you before you even take the first step toward flight.

Sound familiar? If so, I want you to grab hold of the following truth:

No one has created a life of one's dreams
by fulfilling the wishes of others.

You may be motivated to please others or look for fulfillment through external affirmation, but do not let go of your dream or your vision simply because someone says it's impossible. You have the tools and the resources within yourself to help make your dreams a reality.

THE THREE FACETS OF CONSCIOUSNESS

Every experience, every conversation, and every reaction to each circumstance in your life is recorded, registered, and played back to you in your mind.

Sometimes this constant replay results in a negative outcome. It may keep you from turning your dreams into reality. It may not allow your dreams to manifest.

Believe it or not, much of this happens without conscious thought. Our responses to our situations are subconscious. The way we live our lives, the people we associate with, and the input they give us form the belief systems we cultivate within ourselves—and these beliefs form the habits and responses we live by. Naturally, sometimes this is good and sometimes it is bad.

The opinions of others are stored and ready for automatic playback. We don't even have to think about a response. We simply act from our previous conditioning—and all conditioning begins and ends with our subconscious.

For example, if you had a bad experience in a relationship, that experience is stored. Then, when you meet someone new, any behaviors similar to those you experienced in the past will cause the old ones to be replayed, and the behaviors will seem like "red flags" in your new relationship. Your subconscious has a memory of the previous relationship, and similar events act as triggers.

But shouldn't a relationship be based on the present and not the past? As you might expect, the subconscious does not let go of memories or conditioning very easily.

The only way to shake off the old way of thinking, to purge your subconscious mind, is to diligently reprogram your responses. *You* decide what is useful to store and *you* decide what is detrimental to your growth and well-being.

Essentially, your subconscious is storing, playing, and developing new habits that etch grooves in the brain and, just like with an old record player, the needle gets stuck and plays the same old tune over and over. You know the feeling of being stuck in a rut, and that is essentially what's happening when you just follow the leading of your subconscious. It's the same old song.

Your habits can be useful to your well-being as you grow and develop, but they aren't always useful. You have to consciously decide which tunes you want to play, when, and how.

Does your taste in music change over the years? Your clothes? Your preferences for foods and environments? These are all external. Doesn't it make sense, then, that your habits should also change over time?

Habits are internal, and internal changes tend to be more challenging than external changes. If the correct habits are made permanent, they can change the course of your life when applied correctly. External changes—like a bigger car, a promotion, a brand-new house—can sometimes give a false sense of progress, but external changes very rarely have any effect on habits or conditioning.

Understand and apply this:

Changing your habits is the essence of behavior change.

Changing your behavior requires changing your attitudes toward the situations and circumstances you encounter in life. Change in attitude and change in behavior go hand in hand.

It comes back to you! *You* have the choice to create your own reality in the deep recesses of your subconscious, ready for playback. Creating your own reality allows you to live your life on your terms and manifest your vision for *you*.

Going with the flow of past conditioning can do only one thing: keep you tied to the status quo. The cold, hard truth that affects us all is this:

Our state of mind affects our outer reality.

Really let that sink in. We all live primarily in the conscious state: we feel and see things on an everyday level and are influenced by them. This includes everything that we can touch, taste, smell, see, and hear. Our senses are, by definition, restricted to the body. The body and the senses are inextricably tied to our conscious state, so we tend to believe that everything around us is real.

As a result, when we allow our imaginations to soar and when we believe that things are possible, the superconscious mind takes over because it deals exclusively in the limitless realms of possibility.

When you are not in the conscious state, you are not limited by your senses. You are unlimited. There is no reference point to yourself as a being who is sentient (having the power of perception by the senses) in the realm of the imagination. Your senses don't limit you in any way.

This concept of three facets of consciousness—the subconscious, conscious, and superconscious—is vital to your understanding of the importance of imagination. If you fail to realize that you are working to move yourself forward in three different areas of reality at all times, you are essentially failing your life's vision.

You have to get all three facets of consciousness working together, much like a symphony, to reach the potential of your life's vision.

Vision is the aspect of yourself that allows you to find your purpose, but you can move forward only when you understand that you are an integrated being. You are not trying to manifest into reality only one aspect of yourself. You have many different facets that require full integration.

One example of this internal complexity is our possession of a human nature and a divine nature. The superconscious state allows deeper realizations to percolate from the spiritual or divine part of our nature; we can then manifest them into reality, if we allow this process to occur.

However, if we exist only on the single human plane, we can only bring to pass (manifest into reality) that which seems very tangible. The difference is that our imagination presents intangible possibilities that are waiting to be acted upon and manifested into reality. This process is often referred to as *innovation*.

You need to be the originator and innovator of the plan of action in your life. You are hardwired that way. Don't you want to act upon your life and not have your life act upon you? Don't you want to be proactive, not reactive?

Without question, you want to breathe deeply and become fully intoxicated by the elixir of your divine nature being expressed, soaring to heights that exceed your wildest imagination!

Here lies a deep and profound truth:

> *Do your part and you will be astounded at the outcome.*

For example, everyone knows of the great "I Have a Dream" speech by Martin Luther King Jr. When he gave the speech, do you think he envisioned that America would one day have a black president? Probably not—but he took action on his own dream, and that dream had its own impact on American society as a whole.

You can do the same. King's dream was not tangible at the time, but through much effort he was connected to it, he felt it, and it was his passion. He was connected to it internally, and this internal connection moved him emotionally and motivated him until the dream was manifested into reality by his human effort.

The dream came from his superconscious or divine spiritual awareness. The manifestation of his dream was a combination of the superconscious, conscious, and subconscious all integrating and working together to bring about a beautiful symphony of vision becoming reality.

King's subconscious self-talk conditioning did not talk him out of pursuing his vision. Rather, his superconscious and subconscious were in sync, and the result was the manifestation of his dream to reality. It was a conscious realization of a dream. This is full integration at work—*and you can accomplish the same!*

CHAPTER 2

Turn *intangible* dreams into *tangible* reality through intuition.

We all want to live extraordinary lives. We all want to make the best contributions to our family, work, and elsewhere. To do so requires an integration of intangible dreams with tangible reality.

The shift needs to happen … but that is where the disconnect begins for most people.

As we imagine an event or a situation, many things come into play. Our emotions are triggered, our fears begin to arise, our self-talk begins to talk us out of certain possibilities, and our logic begins to take over. When this happens, we lose the most important aspect of ourselves that could have helped us make our dreams come true.

This is a very natural reaction, yet its crippling power is often underestimated.

What happens is that the subconscious mind automatically selects stored files that have never been deleted from our memory banks. When we subconsciously press the Search button for situations and circumstances that are similar to what we are facing, the subconscious mind goes to these preexisting, automatic default settings.

Wouldn't you rather the Search button download new software that would actually help you shift into a new way of thinking? Of course you would! We all would—but it's not going to happen unless you deliberately choose it.

The superconscious state, one of the three states of consciousness, comes back into play with the manifestation of your purpose. Because the superconscious state is where all creativity originates, it is responsible for the feeling, intuition, and sense that there is something happening that you cannot explain.

LEARNING TO TUNE IN TO YOUR INTUITION

Have you ever had the feeling that something just wasn't right? You couldn't put your finger on it, but you felt uneasy about something or someone. Looking back, maybe you said, *I knew something was off about that individual, but I didn't listen to myself. I pursued the situation anyway.*

Sound familiar? We've all had those feelings that we look back on and say, *I wish I had listened to my feelings.*

On the opposite end of the spectrum, maybe we wish we had acted upon something or taken advantage of a good opportunity. We missed a really great opportunity and may say something like, *I knew I should have acted upon that. I just had that feeling.* But the opportunity passed us by.

I often describe the process of manifesting anything in our lives as *magic* or *alchemy*. One definition of alchemy, originating from ancient times, is simply a magical power or process transmuting base metals to gold—a transmutation of the seemingly impossible to the possible.

There is magic or alchemy resident in your imagination. You have the ability to bring forth your vision into reality. That magical power is *intuition*. It is the feeling that something is possible; it is the sense of something greater; it is the understanding of your innate spiritual awareness that requires more expression of yourself in this world. There is no limit.

Don't dismiss your intuition. The intuitive part of the process is the most important to understand when it comes to manifesting vision into reality. To help clarify, substitute the word *vision* for *purpose*. Everyone who has ever been on fire with purpose has had a vision, sparked by the imagination, of what they could accomplish.

This vision prompts them to act from a place of feeling or intuition, does it not? Some people refer to this as a "hunch."

Learning to trust this hunch or intuition is an integral part of developing the skill of listening to the still, small voice that resides inside of you. If you prevent this process from occurring, you feel stifled and unable to connect with yourself or with others at the level you desire.

For most people, this disconnect can manifest as unhappiness, frustration, or lack of energy and drive, and that causes depression. In turn, this depression is a sign that we are out of balance and not at ease with ourselves (dis-at-ease). It's a signal that something needs to be addressed—because that still, small voice inside of us is crying out to be expressed to the world.

If you do not allow that magic to occur and interact with the world, you will sense a disconnect inside of you. This dis-at-ease can also manifest itself as stress, which can cause health issues if continually ignored.

Listening to this voice is a skill; like any other, it needs to be developed and honed so that it's sharp, clear, and precise, so it can be used as intended: to be the guiding voice of your life.

In order to develop a strong sense of intuition:

> *You need to be able to act on the information that you are constantly receiving from inside of you.*

When you begin to discover the blocks that prevent you from acting in your own best interests in all areas of life, you have to ask yourself why.

For most of our lives, we have been conditioned by what other people and society think our lives should be; we filter our words and actions based on how they'll appear to our family, friends, and peers. Our choices are based not on our free will, but upon the input or will of others.

How often are we actually exercising our own free will when establishing our reality? We make choices every single day of our lives, and those choices become the sum total of our existence. Day by day, our lives begin to shift in a certain direction. At some point we begin to realize that maybe the life we have is not the life we want.

Is that not true? Is the life you are living the life you want?

As time goes by, this epiphany becomes more apparent. It can be more pronounced at the midpoint of our lives, which is why it is referred to as a "midlife crisis." We review our life and realize we have come to a place where we did not want to end up. Regardless of the things we thought would bring us fulfillment—education, degree, job, title, fame, etc.—we are at a place where we did not expect to be.

In the years I've been coaching and speaking with executives and people from many different walks of life, there is one recurring theme I hear more than any other. It is this:

I don't know what I want.

The second-most-common theme is related to the first:

I know what I want ... I just don't know how to get it.

Do you know what you want? Do you know how to get what you want?

The solution is to listen to the still, small voice inside of you that is constantly giving you direction.

I know it sounds too simple, but hear me out. That still, small voice is creating a vision for you to see, giving you directions to follow, and activating your imagination so that you can act upon it. The need to turn intangible dreams into tangible reality is why you even have an imagination to act upon. It acts upon you, and you act upon it, thereby creating a reciprocating energy that manifests the dream to reality.

WHAT'S YOUR DREAM?

At various times in our lives, we all have something we dream about or a vision of how we want our lives to unfold. For example, we might dream of a new career, a vacation, a deeper spiritual life, stronger finances, better health, a new home, more friends, or a new and fulfilling personal relationship.

We can create countless visions, can't we? And the reason we can is that they do not already exist, right? But our mind allows us to preview the possibility of these things happening, doesn't it?

And that proves that it's possible! You can see it. It's a reality that could be yours!

Albert Einstein says it like this:

> *"Imagination is everything. It is the preview of life's coming attractions."*

But if your imagination is activated and you don't participate, no wave of alchemy can occur. "Dead in the water," as they say. The wave of imaginative power crashes to the shore, never to crest again.

Sadly, it remains where most of us leave it—in our minds—and it never manifests itself again.

But we are programmed to have wave after wave of invigorating, intoxicating, inspiring, and enthusiastic energy to carry out the vision we have been given! It's within each of us to dream and to achieve. It's there!

It's essential to understand that your vision leads to your mission and your purpose—what you were born to do, just like your DNA imprint was there before your birth. Your physical manifestation of self is simply the correct design that allows you to accomplish it. You just have to see it.

OWN YOUR OWN VISION

In order for your vision to become reality, you must have a deep sense of self, one that comes from self-analysis. To own your vision, you must spend the time to know yourself, to understand yourself, to realize that what you want is important and that your vision is important.

When you own your vision and act upon it, you own your own life.

Your vision is what you want. If it creates a deep emotional response in you, you will be able to sustain the energy to see your vision manifested. This process of introspection will also allow you to discover how you lead yourself and to understand your strengths and challenges.

Addressing your strengths and challenges will define your personal leadership. How will you lead yourself where you want to go? No one else will lead you there. It is up to you.

Seeing what you want, knowing it, owning it, feeling your vision, seeing your dream in the very depths of your soul and knowing how to lead yourself there, and then pursuing it with passion—these are the very essence of personal leadership. Dial down the negative self-talk. Tuning in to your intuition and unleashing your imagination will guide you in your journey and help you realize your vision.

> *When your vision and passion ignite, you*
> *are on fire!*

CHAPTER 3

Effective communication–your self-talk–matters *more* than you think!

Martin Luther King Jr. gives us an illustration of effective self-talk. His passion ignited his vision, and the result was the manifestation of the dream to reality. Whatever your vision might be, the principle is the same.

It goes without saying that the pursuit of a vision should never be done to the detriment of someone else; the vision must always take into account morals and character. A true vision will result in a meaningful life, one that brings joy and happiness. In many ways, a vision becomes its holder's moral compass.

Of course, history is full of examples of people with visions that were selfish, self-centered, and damaging to humanity—most decidedly not for the greater good. These negative visions, however, were not sustainable and left no lasting beneficial effects.

Likewise, history has many positive examples of people with visions that *were* for the greater good of humanity. These left an indelible imprint for many years, even centuries, after the individual departed this existence.

Many people—saints, businessmen, leaders, politicians, and social reformers—have seen, felt, and been inspired by something inside of them that propelled them forward toward their mission.

THE IMPORTANCE OF SELF-ANALYSIS

Deep introspection—self-analysis—is incredibly powerful when we use it to uncover why we feel it is impossible to realize a certain vision or dream. Through introspection, we may discover that one of the limiting reasons is our self-doubt.

Why don't people accomplish their dreams? Is it because their dreams are impossible? No. Is it because they don't possess the innate, God-given ability to reach those dreams? No.

The truth is, each of us is unique and blessed with abilities and talents. And if a vision can be conceived, it can be achieved!

So, what is the real reason that people do not accomplish their dreams?

> *The real reasons people don't fulfill their dreams: conditioning, self-doubt, and the overuse of logic.*

THE ROLE OF EFFECTIVE COMMUNICATION

Effective communication is one of the most important aspects of living our lives to the fullest. You might be wondering, "What does effective communication have to do with vision?"

Like two well-greased cogs, effective communication and alchemy fit together perfectly, creating the magic of making your visions come true. They ignite your purpose.

Communication through self-talk means affirming consistently, all day long, what you believe about yourself. Self talk manifests into reality your vision and purpose— or the lack thereof. After all, self-talk can be positive or negative.

Thought is communication within yourself. Your every thought ignites your ability to manifest into the conscious realm your dreams, your wishes, and your hopes in every area of your life.

Every thought that has no limit originates from a place that can't be fully understood—it's from the superconscious state, the state of mind that knows no limits. Once you have had that thought, you immediately begin to have a dialogue with yourself. That constant internal conversation about your thought from the superconscious state begins to create images in your mind that trigger your imagination.

That conversation with yourself can be the beginning or the end of your magic. You talk yourself into or out of your own dreams!

Effective communication has everything to do with how effectively you communicate with yourself.

PLENTY OF BAD PRESS

Nothing can or will be accomplished if you talk badly about yourself to yourself. Believe me, there are more than enough people out there who will be happy to fill that role for you—to constantly voice limiting, negative, small-minded thoughts about you. And if you decide to leave the status quo and establish your life based upon your own subconscious programming, people will come out of the woodwork to hurl their minimizing words at you.

You don't need them! And you don't need your own negative words—do you?

We are all self-fulfilling prophecies. The outcomes of our lives are determined by our ability to navigate the bombardment of ongoing dialogue in our heads about the situations, circumstances, and people in our lives.

Your life and mine are basically formed on two alternating situations: 1) what happens to us, and 2) how we respond to what happens.

Interestingly, this internal dialogue—as we deal with what happens and decide how to respond—creates emotions, which in turn create reactions. These reactions grow to become the environment around us and, more importantly, the environment we create within ourselves.

We can either *respond*, by controlling our emotions and remaining calm, or we can *react*. When our emotions drive a reaction, it does not usually end well! Respond or react—the difference is in the degree of self-talk.

But do you know why you react? What caused the emotions that you felt? Good questions—and this is one of the greatest challenges in personal leadership. Being able to understand the reasons that you react to certain situations or people, and bringing those emotions under control, is personal leadership at its best.

CHANGING THE EMOTIONS

When emotions have less of an effect, we begin to gain a different perspective. This creates a different reaction, physically as well as mentally, which in turn affects our internal dialogue. This change in dialogue allows us to be more objective in our response and obtain a better result for everyone, ourselves included.

Isn't that what we all want—better results and outcomes for every situation we are involved in?

No doubt we have all been in situations where we reacted in a certain way or said something we wished we had not. It was not because we wanted to, but our emotions dictated to us the way we behaved and spoke.

If we apply the old rule of "count to ten," simply take a deep breath, or walk away until we are calm again, we will automatically begin to realize a clearer, deeper sense of ourselves communicating from a different place with a different outcome. These are simple tools that anyone can use, but they are very effective in beginning to change old behavior patterns.

Changing behavior has a way of bringing about change in our own dialogue, and that changes the outcome in life.

This change is deep and profound on so many levels that we feel an empowerment beginning to develop within us, a sense of strength we have not felt before that comes from self-discipline. We are not allowing our emotions to run us—we are running them!

As you gain more control over yourself, you become more in control of your future, and everything becomes clearer because your destiny is in your own hands. The attainment of your future begins and ends with your ability to master yourself and to be focused and mindful of your personal leadership.

This, of course, affects your professional leadership, because personal and professional leadership are inextricably intertwined. How many times have you seen a great career brought to a screeching halt, not because the individual could not perform professionally, but because he or she simply had poor *personal* leadership and judgment? It happens all the time. The ability to perform the tasks of a job is known as a "hard" skill, while having the personality and good judgment to get along with yourself and others is thought of as a "soft" skill. You need both kinds of skills to be successful in realizing your vision to reality.

As I have mentioned before, this success requires deep self-analysis and introspection to begin to unravel the ball of string that has been tied up in knots for so long that it has hindered us from expressing ourselves in an effective and rewarding way so that we can live full and meaningful lives.

How you communicate with yourself directly affects how you communicate with others and how successful you are at reaching your desires, goals, and dreams. If you are constantly frustrated and angry with yourself or with circumstances in your life, you will project that energy onto everything and everyone around you. Remember this:

Everything you desire depends upon your inner dialogue and your attitude about the circumstances of your life.

Your self-confidence, and your ability to convey your dreams and vision to others in an effective and competent manner, depend upon your relationship with yourself. It keeps coming back to that.

In fact, your self-esteem, self-confidence, and self-image are all connected to how you communicate. The tonality of your voice, your eye contact, and your body language are all messages that everyone you meet is aware of, whether consciously or subconsciously. These traits form their perception of you and are all directly correlated to how you feel about yourself. Not everyone is going to think you're wonderful, but if you have enough self-confidence, it won't make any difference to you or deter you from your outcome.

I am not talking about arrogance. You know the difference. When people go above and beyond to help you, they are responding to your charisma and confidence as you work together in concert. When people do things begrudgingly and do the absolute minimum to appease you, you may have some arrogance that needs to be addressed.

We are back to your personal leadership.

LEADING COMES FROM INSPIRATION

How you lead yourself will determine how you lead others. If you can lead others successfully, they will follow you. If they follow you, they can help you achieve your dreams. Your ability to communicate effectively allows you to surround yourself with people who can help you make your vision come true, for nothing is accomplished alone.

People are drawn to self-confident, self-motivated visionaries. Visionaries possess a contagious enthusiasm and are a wellspring of inspiration and ingenuity. They are able to adjust their behaviors, communication style, and attitude to the constantly changing situations and circumstances that are inevitable in the pursuit of any dream.

The word *enthusiasm* comes from Greek origins. The *en* means "in" and *theos* means "deity or spirit," with a literal translation of "carrying the spirit within." Another translation for the Greek word *enthousiasmos* is "divine inspiration." I like that!

Inspiration is the fuel to the fire of imagination. Inspiration allows a continual flow of creativity to give you the ideas you need to execute your vision. Many obstacles will come your way that need to be overcome in order for you to realize your dreams.

With inspiration, obstacles and problems are simply opportunities. But without the ability to access inspiration, you will simply be lost, like a ship without a rudder, as soon as a crisis threatens to thwart your aspirations.

To use the inspiring sentiment of Abraham Maslow, if the only tool in your toolbox for dealing with crisis is a hammer, then every issue becomes a nail. The true essence of inspiration is allowing yourself to flow through every situation expecting a positive outcome, seeking a resolution in a calm and collected manner, allowing space for intuition to enter your consciousness and spark your inspiration, guiding you to the correct action for the resolution you require. Inspiration unlocks the whole toolbox for you!

The process of allowing space for intuition is different for everyone. You need to find the process that works best for you. The process itself should lead you back to the original suggestion of deep introspection, self-analysis, and self-knowledge. Learn how to draw on the inexhaustible wellspring of inspiration, creativity, and awareness. This enables you to respond to any given situation rather than allowing it to act upon you.

Notice I didn't say *react*, but *respond*.

You are the one acting, you are the one in charge—and that makes you the one who is responding!

You will then be able to strategize, look at all the possibilities and outcomes, and consult with the individuals that you have gathered around you—those who believe in you and your vision because of your effective communication skills, enthusiasm, and the ability to inspire them to help you reach your goal. That will get you the results you want!

MOVE FORWARD!

Accessing creativity and inspiration is a vital part of innovation, which you'll need in order to move forward with any new vision supplied by your superconscious state.

Any alchemy or magic in your life requires an innovative mind-set without fear or doubt. You cannot create from a place of fear, because fear paralyzes. The natural flow of energy in your body ceases when it is surrounded by fear. Many people are familiar with the acronym FEAR: false evidence appearing real. Don't let it rule in any way in your life.

When you imagine—when you see a possibility in your mind's eye—you are being prompted to live your own possibilities. Your unlimited superconscious is speaking loud and clear ... but so is your programmed, limited, and conditioned subconscious mind. The battle rages!

You *must* pursue your dreams, set new goals, and make unique contributions to your own life and the lives of others. You *should* be free in your own expression of self, and you should experience the depth of your being in that expression, for it is through expression that you feel alive, able, and capable.

CHAPTER 4

Live with positive expectancy, *access* your intuition, and *develop* courage.

Wouldn't you agree that when we are filled with fresh vitality and enthusiasm, our relationships also improve?

Likewise, if we stifle our own freedom and expression, we feel like a constricted garden hose with a kink in it. We all know how effective one little kink can be in stifling the flow of water; it's the same with our flow of intuition and imagination.

The answer is to fix the kink. Get the water flowing again. If only we could just straighten ourselves out to flow freely!

LET FREEDOM RING!

The good news is that it is possible to get the kinks out of your own life! And when you do, you ignite a series of events that release in you and your environment an enormous amount of life force. People will just appear who will help you, synchronistic events will begin to happen, and alchemy and magic will take place in your life!

All great achievements started with an idea, dream, or vision; it was acted upon, and people came to assist the outcome, simply because someone had the courage to act.

Did you ever wonder where all those necessary people came from? How the events just "happened"? Nobody had it all planned out. The visionary was living under correct knowledge and acted on the vision with inspiration and creativity … and the rest is history!

So what does "living under correct knowledge" really mean? To investigate this further, we would have to look deeply once again into the first state of consciousness: the superconscious. We have to understand where all real knowledge comes from. Simply put, we cannot live under correct knowledge unless we recognize the source of all wisdom and guidance.

Correct knowledge propels us forward—not in a haphazard fashion but in a sustained, intelligent, and distinct way. There is a definite plan and a definite guidance that moves us, touches us, and speaks to us. The intuitive process is one of the sources of knowledge that we can act on.

You may be thinking, "That sounds good, but how am I supposed to act on a process that usually defies the logic in my life?"

Intuition requires action from a place of faith, not logic. And because faith and intuition go hand in hand, you have to develop both muscles effectively in order to accomplish your dreams.

What is faith? It has a spiritual connotation and entails believing in something you cannot see. Yes, this defies explanation, but it has a profound effect on your life. Faith is essentially believing in forces unseen. Whenever you reach a situation that is beyond your ability to resolve it, then by default you have to turn inward and find strength within yourself to move forward with positive expectancy, right? This is faith.

POSITIVE EXPECTANCY

Ponder this question for a moment: Is there a difference between what you expect to receive in life and what you think might happen?

Of course there is. I strongly suggest that you act differently toward what you *expect* to happen than you do toward what you *think* may happen. Why? Simply because it is natural to also consider that something may *not* happen. There is an easy transition between thinking something may happen and thinking that it may not happen—but a posture of expectation is very different. Consider this:

It is easier to change your mind about
what you think than what you expect.

We all tend to meet or exceed our own expectations. But we don't do this when it applies to what we *think* of ourselves, only what we *expect* of ourselves. There is a subtle difference, and the mind knows it. Give the mind an out, and it will run for the exit.

What is the difference in these two statements?

1) "I did not think that was going to happen."

2) "I did not expect that to happen."

The first statement is logical, and logic is all about thinking, so by default you will look for a logical, thinking resolution to the issue. The mind automatically will begin to think about what happened. Haven't you been there and done that yourself?

You think, "If only I had not done that, if I had thought about it, maybe I could have avoided the situation. Maybe

I'll think through the next situation more deeply before I commit."

Sound familiar? Ever had that dialogue with yourself?

So what's the alternative? If you did not *expect* it to happen, your expectation was met. The mind will automatically find a way to try to have an expectation met because what you expect has an element of self-worth and self-confidence attached to it.

For example, you may say to yourself, "There is no way I expect to be treated that way," but would you ever say, "There is no way I think I should be treated that way"? Of course not! Don't you know how you want to be treated? Of course you do. It's not something you really need to *think* about. You already know.

Expectation suggests an element of knowing, while thinking suggests an element of doubt.

For example, imagine that someone gave you an orange. You ate the orange, and it was not particularly sweet, but it was the only orange you had ever eaten. You would probably think that all oranges were like that, slightly bitter and not overly sweet.

However, if you had previously sampled ripe, hand-picked oranges, you would *know* that all oranges are not bitter, and naturally your expectation would be quite different.

Here is my point: When you know something about yourself from in-depth introspection and from facing different situations out of your comfort zone so that you can grow (this is known as a "stretch goal"), what you think and know about yourself will change—and so will your expectations of yourself. You know yourself and what you are capable of, so you do not *think* you can do something— you *know* it.

Consider the following statements. Which exudes more self-confidence, self-worth, and self-esteem?

1. I *know* I can do this.

2. I *think* I can do this.

The difference is clear! When you state—to others and yourself—what you expect, that produces a different energy from trying to convince someone of what you think.

> *A dream becomes a reality because you expect it to, not because you think it might happen.*

Positive expectancy allows you to have faith. It gives you a vision of dreams fulfilled. It propels and motivates you. It excites you and keeps you focused.

This is one of the aspects of living with correct "knowledge." Not "think-ledge." And without a doubt, you *know* the difference.

ACCESSING YOUR INTUITION

Intuition gives us the sense of something to act upon with positive expectancy, but how do we access our intuition? And how do we know the difference between the feeling that is guiding us, our logic, and our ego?

The intuitive process deals specifically with our feelings. It is those deep feelings that give us the sense that there is something we need to do. That sense persists and never leaves us. We can't shake it, and that is what helps create our vision for the future.

Intuition provides us with a constant flow of information. It works from a deep sense of feeling within us, and it gives us the ability to be in touch with our feelings and our intuition.

Women are often considered more intuitive than men—hence the term "women's intuition." Despite that idea, I believe that anyone can access his or her intuition. Intuition is not gender specific.

Accessing our intuition first requires us to get into a calm state of mind, what I refer to as a "flat space" of response. This involves not allowing too many outside influences to act upon us, so that we can receive a sense of the right direction or action to take.

Intuition is an exciting and beautiful experience. We all know that when we are in pain or need healing, getting into nature and finding a quiet place to sit will give us some peace and rest. We don't know exactly what happens as we enjoy this space, but we feel a calming, healing peace that comes from being in that environment. It is a feeling that is stirred inside of us. It has no logic or reason; it just is. It exists in and of itself. We connect to something in nature that somehow resonates within us and brings us back to ourselves.

Similarly, intuition is essentially connecting yourself to yourself through the source of all creation and receiving information through that connection that is individually yours to act upon.

LISTEN TO YOURSELF

When you receive information intuitively, you feel something. This feeling can save you from spending an inordinate amount of time and energy pursuing situations and circumstances that will not serve you well.

Most likely, however, you don't stop long enough to listen to this intuitive guidance. You probably live a frantic life, seldom pausing for more than sixty seconds to take a breath, to slow down, and to feel. Right?

But if you don't slow down or take time to feel, how do you truly know how to listen to your inner voice when all you have to guide yourself is constant outer chatter?

Have you ever been told, "You know what to do, you're just not listening to yourself"? If so, do you know what that really means?

Perhaps you have experienced the ramifications of not listening to yourself. Maybe you didn't follow that still, small voice. What did it cost you?

Looking back, we can all think of the many times when we failed to listen to ourselves. And if we were to honestly calculate the lost time and energy that could have been put into more useful pursuits, we would be amazed. We should have listened to ourselves!

We should never forget:

> *Intuition is the ability to pay attention to your feelings, trust them, and act upon them.*

Your feelings have meaning. They may not be tangible, but they do lead to a tangible and meaningful outcome.

Intuition is profound and comes from a very deep source within us, and we must pay attention to it. The manifestation of our purpose and our dreams depends on it! Our intuition allows us to act on our hunches—the feelings of something being right or wrong—and we have to follow these hunches to manifest what we want.

To listen to your intuition, you must spend time in quiet solitude. Stillness provides answers. It is that flat place I mentioned where we get out of our own way and allow something greater to work with us in our lives. We are not meant to do everything by ourselves. There is help and inner guidance available 24/7 if only we can be still enough to listen.

It doesn't have to be a lot of time, either. But do try to allocate as much time as your life and schedule will allow. You may have to change some habits, behaviors, and attitudes to accommodate this paradigm shift in your life if you're not already doing so.

Intuition is another tool that must be developed and used in the manifestation of your dreams. This is another aspect of what I call LUCK: living under correct knowledge.

IT TAKES COURAGE

It has been said many times: courage requires that you go out on a limb—that's where the fruit is!

An often-overlooked element for manifesting your dreams into reality is the simple requirement of living life courageously. We need courage so that we can act on our greatest desires and so we can let go of places, people, and situations that no longer serve us.

Whenever we try to move forward, there is an element within us, fueled by fear, that rises up and says, *what if* this and *what if* that. It's the "what if" syndrome. Ever been there?

Let's take a look at our earlier acronym, FEAR: false evidence appearing real. Isn't that what the "what if" syndrome is all about? It's fear, and it's not even real! There really is no evidence to support the "what if" story playing out in your mind. The entire "what if" scenario is, by definition, a perpetually impossible situation.

The only outcome of "what if" is this: possibilities perpetually paralyzed. Isn't that what fear does? It paralyzes any forward motion toward an outcome because your imagination puts up pictures of failure and you talk yourself out of taking action toward what you want.

Don't let that happen! Take the antidote:

The antidote to fear is courage.

No doubt you have found yourself at a place in life where you knew you needed to make some changes—you felt it deeply in your soul—but the act of actually making those changes ... that's big! That's the turning point where change really takes place, and courage is required.

It is at this pivotal point where you realize that manifesting your true life into existence will establish your own personal identity, putting your own fingerprint on your existence. This turning point is crucial to your understanding that in order for you to have an impact on others, you are forced to make an impact on your own life first.

This is personal leadership at its core. But it's not going to just happen. You must choose it, and that takes courage.

The type of courage you need is the courage that comes from knowing yourself, your own personality, and how you relate to yourself. Because courage is as individual as you are, what may be a courageous act to one person may not be brave to another. And courage has differing levels of tolerance to risk versus security.

Have you ever been served something at a restaurant that was not quite what you ordered? Did you debate whether to return it, eat it, or even leave the restaurant?

To some people, it is an act of courage just to speak up, while for others that act wouldn't be courageous in the least. But the person who has no problem with speaking up at a restaurant may not have the courage it takes to leave everything behind and start a business.

Each person has his or her own degree of courage. You simply need to know what level of personal courage you are comfortable with, and this comes from self-analysis and introspection. Consider these: Are you comfortable assuming all the risk in a situation like a business venture? Would you feel more comfortable sharing that risk with a business partner? Are you the type of person who likes to discuss ideas with people before you execute a strategy? Or are you happier and more comfortable when you make all the decisions yourself, thereby assuming all responsibility for the outcome?

You know yourself—*know*, not *think*—and you understand what motivates you internally for you to manifest externally the vision of your future. You need to know how much risk you are comfortable taking on in order to achieve your desired outcome.

Acts of heroism are usually extraordinary acts of courage in adverse situations. But we are not really talking here about extraordinary acts of courage. We simply need to consistently, on a daily basis, be able to access our own center of courage. This involves acting consistently and courageously with faith every single day.

It is in this consistency, using the muscles of courage and faith, that you begin to displace all doubt and fear. As you begin to see the results of your actions from a place of strength, of positive expectancy, then you will begin to act automatically in the manner that brings the greatest results in your life.

The courage you need is based on your value system and personal and professional goals. You'll see that this means stepping out of the status quo into your own new paradigm. It means reprogramming the conditioning that you have been led to believe. It means assessing and reassessing your environment, your friends, and the influences that are continually affecting you.

All of this requires courage. It requires personal leadership. It requires character and credibility. And it takes courage to say and do the things that will take you where you want to go. The manifestation of your vision, the moving of it to reality, requires courage, commitment, and conviction.

Without courage, you will never be able to savor the ripe fruit of all your extraordinary accomplishments. Sometimes you have to go out on a limb because that's where the fruit is!

CHAPTER 5

Your personal *culture* will determine how
your dreams and goals are manifested.

Establishing or reestablishing your environment and
social structure will greatly enable you to create and
live your dreams and enjoy the fruits of your labor.

The social structure that you have created allows you to
express yourself on your terms, in your world, with people
who support you and help you. This social structure can be
called your own *personal culture*.

WHAT DO YOU STAND FOR?

Show me your friends and I will tell you who you are.
For example, you may have, at some point in your life, been
more interested in going out with friends, partying, and

being involved in conversations that at the time were very interesting.

But over time, your needs and requirements—your social environment—may have changed. Your original personal culture was one of socialization and going out. This is enjoyable and, of course, there is nothing wrong with that personal culture, but people change over time.

You may have decided that you wanted to be less social and more introspective and quiet, reading more books and enjoying the discussion of different topics with new friends in your newfound space or personal culture.

Whatever your personal culture is, it should be reflected in your social structure and environments; your lifestyle should express your personal values and goals. This allows an alignment between your environment and who you are.

When you grow and change (which we all need to do in order to feel fulfilled and satisfied), there may be a natural change in long-established relationships and environments. This culture shift can be difficult on a personal as well as a professional level.

If an organization wants a culture shift, they go through the same process that you do. I've helped organizations move from one culture to another and it's a process that truly requires commitment, resolve, and courage. It is no different with shifting from one personal culture to another.

LINING THINGS UP

It is much easier to reach your goals and fulfill your dreams when you create a life that is in sync with your own culture. As you change, so should your personal culture. You should always know what you stand for and who you want to surround yourself with … or you will fall for anything.

The power of influence is not to be underestimated! If you want to grow and develop, surround yourself with the people you admire. They may have achieved their goals or may be in the process of achieving them, but they possess attributes, attitudes, and behaviors that you would like in your own life. This will give you the support, encouragement, and motivation you'll need when the going gets tough. People who have been where you are trying to go can share with you inspirational stories of how they overcame some of the obstacles and challenges that you face. Learning from their experiences can give you a shortcut to the resolution of many issues. Their example is an inspiration.

Shortcuts such as these are invaluable, for they save time and effort. They keep you from traveling down roads that are completely unnecessary. Avoid those wrong roads by listening to people who have the directions to where you want to go.

If your personal culture does not change with your need to grow and develop, then when you hit a seemingly impossible obstacle, where will you go for advice, support, and direction? Naturally, you will turn to the people you have around you! But if they are not moving in the same or a similar direction as you are, how can they advise you? If they have no experience and don't know where they are going … it will be the blind leading the blind!

It is not blindness you seek. Rather, you want a clear vision. You must have people in your personal culture who can help keep you focused.

HOW TO STAY FOCUSED

You cannot picture anything if you are out of focus. That's the way it works, for creating a vision for your life requires a very clear focus.

Ever tried to take a sharp picture with a camera that was out of focus? It simply cannot be done. You can use all the special effects you want, but the picture will be worthless without clear focus. Likewise, you cannot bring a vision to reality without clear and concise focus.

Focusing on anything allows it to expand and grow. That is why concentrated focus is so powerful. Consider the laser beam. From home improvement projects (straight lines) to weapons (firepower) to surgery (accurate and precise cuts), the laser gets the job done with incredible precision. There is no "close enough" with a laser. It's right on target!

Similarly, concentrated focus gives you greater productivity. Is there not a huge difference between being *busy* and being *productive*? What is your definition of productivity? Is it the hours worked in a day or the accomplishment of certain priorities?

> *Busy people never seem to have enough*
> *time. Isn't that right? But productive*
> *people find ways to get things done, don't*
> *they?*

Productivity requires you to understand what your priorities are—and when you focus on your priorities, you will get things done! You will have not only the results you want, but also a great sense of accomplishment because you are consistently moving toward the manifestation of your vision. It is in the attainment of your goals and vision that you gain the most happiness and satisfaction in your life.

We all feel good and more satisfied when we have had a productive and positive day. Usually that means that we accomplished what we set out and scheduled to do that day.

Imagine focusing every day on what you set out to do by correct prioritization. The days will turn into weeks and the weeks will turn into months. As the years go by, you will see the attainment of your vision formulated by concise, well-thought-out goals that match your vision and your personal values, followed by a plan of action that includes strategic focus and a clear set of scheduled priorities.

STRATEGIC FOCUS FOR GOAL COMPLETION

So what is strategic focus? This type of focus promotes the creation of a strategy to help you complete your goals.

The most successful people, who make up a small 3 percent of the population, are successful in part because they have written clear, concise goals that include a strategy for their implementation.

The importance of strategy in goal setting is crucial. Though many consider goal setting to be only getting from point A to point B, the truth is that along the way in the accomplishment of any goal there will be obstacles—some obvious and some not so obvious.

If we focus only on getting from point A to point B, we may overlook the importance of each individual step that needs to be carefully planned and prepared for along the way.

A strategy allows you to plan each step, to reevaluate, and to make sure you are not so deeply entrenched in going from A to B that you overlook the important details in the attainment of your goal.

For example, one of your goals may be to buy a new home in a different neighborhood. You accomplish that goal only to find that there were plans to build a highway behind the home you just bought. Part of the strategy in the attainment of your home should have been doing the relevant research regarding new development scheduled in the area.

Imagine having to decide whether you wanted to live with the freeway behind your house or to move again. Neither option is a win for you. However, if part of your strategy for going from A to B had been detailed research on the proposed area, you would never have moved there in the first place.

Another example is the desire to lose weight. You could just start an exercise program as most do. Say you weigh 140 pounds and want to reduce your weight to 115. I have heard this kind of goal many times. Sound familiar?

Whatever your goal, just starting on it is not the answer. It pays to plan.

Before you read any further, grab a notepad and write down some of the strategies you will need to implement so that you can accomplish this health goal of losing weight. That's the A-to-B goal, but what strategies do you need to implement?

Here are ten questions you would need to answer to formulate a strategy:

1. How do I accurately measure my calories?

2. Does my heart rate affect the amount of calories burned?

3. How many calories can I effectively burn in one hour?

4. How many hours a week can I exercise?

5. How many calories will I burn during the hours I exercise?

6. How do I measure my current resting heart rate?

7. How important is it that I assess my current state of health and conditioning?

8. From this assessment, what realistic expectations can I have over the next month?

9. With my current schedule, how can I implement an effective, realistic exercise program to meet my goal?

10. What diet do I need to implement to attain the results?

Your questions may be different. That's fine, but your questions form your strategy.

ONE BITE AT A TIME

Another important part of accomplishing anything worthwhile is not trying to do too much at once. With the example of the weight-loss goal, you would want to take one of the ten steps and do that one thing for the first week (or within some other time frame you've established). Even if you complete the task ahead of schedule, do not try to move to the next step. Allow yourself extra time to do something you will enjoy. Reward yourself for what you've accomplished. You have started your strategy!

Let's say you gave yourself three days to find the answer to the first question on your list, but you completed your research in one day. What should you do? It's tempting to proceed to the next question immediately, but don't. Stick with your schedule—which means you proceed to the next question on the fourth day. This allows you to feel relaxed and paced, not harried and stressed. You will still complete your goal in the allotted time.

We all operate more effectively when we have time to breathe, reflect, and relax as we move forward in each stage of the accomplishment of our goals. This also gives us time to contemplate, enjoy, and celebrate each step that we accomplish. And perhaps as we contemplate the next step, we are inspired with new insights as to how we would like to proceed with the information we received from answering the first question.

This may sound like common sense, but you'd be surprised how often common sense is lacking when it comes to goal attainment. When I ask the question, "What is your strategy for reaching your desired goal?" I usually get a blank stare.

Now that you have your questions and strategy, you know what I'm talking about!

SMART GOALS

You may be familiar with the acronym SMART for goal setting: specific, measurable, attainable, realistic, and tangible. (Sometimes the *T* is said to stand for *timely*. I prefer *tangible*, but you can use whatever is most effective for you.)

If you begin to apply this acronym in your daily goal setting and ask yourself the question, "Am I living a SMART life?" you will be in the 3 percent of the population who are indeed living a smart life!

Taking care of the details, being specific, and being proactive by thinking outside of the box in any given situation, circumstance, or goal can save you a lot of time, money, and resources. Would you like to save time, money, and resources? Of course. We would all love to do that!

When you have carefully crafted your strategy, have completed the research, and have the appropriate systems, equipment, and environment in place, your ability to accomplish a goal becomes much more realistic.

Going back to the example of the weight-loss strategy, one piece of equipment you might want to invest in would be a heart-rate monitor that accurately measures both heart rate and calories burned. Some monitors can even automatically download the results to your computer. This way you have an accurate measure of your progress, for the measurement of your progress has to be accurate.

Now the goal of losing twenty-five pounds has a strategy behind it and a helpful tool to implement that strategy.

If you cannot measure your progress along the way to the accomplishment of your goal, you will never know where you are getting off track and what the correction needs to be. Having a measure of your progress allows you to become less discouraged and more motivated.

I often hear discouragement in the voices of people who are trying to lose weight. I ask them, "What was your plan, and how are you measuring your ongoing progress consistently?" Very few have a good answer.

With this goal, as with other goals, we aren't only concerned with the first two or three months. Health is a lifestyle that needs to become a habit, for habits and attitudes change behavior—and behavior change will change our lives.

THE POWER OF CONSISTENCY

Consistency is important in any endeavor. Consistency and persistence combined allow you to get sustainable results—and it goes without saying that you want your desired outcome to be sustainable.

These should always be on our radar:

> *Relaxing and enjoying ourselves with*
> *our families and our friends is good and*
> *necessary, as long as we don't lose sight of*
> *our goals, aspirations, mission, and vision.*

If you have the right environment and people around you, they will help you to stay on track just as they do. You will also realize that by producing the correct personal culture (friends and environment), you will tend to get sidetracked a lot less. That is good, because once you are sidetracked and derailed, it is much harder to get back on track.

The right personal culture will help you stay motivated. Motivation is great, because it's like an engine—once you get moving, the momentum will carry you through. Admittedly, the hardest thing to do is get warmed up, but once you are warmed up, you can go as fast as you want!

Consistently moving toward your goals, with the right personal culture, is a beautiful thing. Without the right culture, you will be fighting burnout, exhaustion, and lack of motivation. These go together to slow you down, which is one of the reasons that you can't—and shouldn't try to—do this alone.

PURSUING EXCELLENCE

It is simply not possible to do everything yourself. Sometimes you may think, "If I want anything done right, I have to do it myself." But everything doesn't have to be perfect!

In fact, one of the definitions of perfect is, "Freedom from fault or defect." My suggestion is to aim for excellence, which is "the quality of being outstanding or extremely good" and to adopt the habit of excellence, not perfection, in everything you do. You cannot be flawless and perfect, but you can try to be excellent in all of your endeavors.

The famous Greek philosopher Aristotle summed it up this way:

> *Excellence is an art won by training and*
> *habituation. We do not act rightly because*

we have virtue or excellence, but we
rather have those because we have acted
rightly. We are what we repeatedly do.
Excellence then is not an act but a habit.

It makes sense that everything you do should be established and then improved upon, but begin to get everything moving in the right direction and improve as you go along. It is easier to work a situation from the benefit of experience and create excellence from that experience than to try to create excellence from the starting gate. Get started, and work as you go.

If there's one piece of advice I would give to those seriously pursuing their goals, it would be this:

Get started and improve upon everything
based on the experiences that you learn
along the way.

Experience allows you to make the correct adjustments, but it only works if you have in place the correct strategy. Strategy is the precursor to allowing the experience to begin and unfold. As you work through the strategy, you will learn from experience what needs to be adjusted.

At the beginning of any project, spend less time considering all the little details and more time considering the strategies you need to put in place to ignite the fire of passion within you.

You can always add more wood to a fire to increase its intensity, but if there is not even a spark to begin with, the wood is irrelevant. Put the spark of your ideas into motion, get your vision from the superconscious to the conscious, and douse any self-doubt with copious amounts of water from an enormous fire hose so that nothing holds you back—and then let the fire rage!

Along the way, let others help you. With your incredible communication skills that you have honed through effective communication with yourself and self-analysis, you will understand your own strengths and challenges. You will have worked on your ability to connect and communicate with others. You will be able to effectively convey your vision and what assistance you need to accomplish it. You can delegate with authority and accountability.

When people buy into you, they buy into your vision and your ability to accomplish it.

Having worked with many different organizations, I know that one of the most difficult things for a leader of a company to get is buy-in from the people within the organization—especially if the change involves any type of culture shift or the implementation of new strategies. This is where effective communication is so important.

This concept also applies to your personal life as you try to move forward, express a new vision of yourself to others, create a new personal culture, or implement new strategies. However, it is not always easy to get buy-in from those around you. That is why you have to believe in yourself, know yourself, and maintain your own positive expectancy of the outcome.

Eventually you will see that by acting in sync with your deepest desires, guided by your intuition, you will get the buy-in and help you need. It will arrive as long as you do not deviate from your vision, and fear will be displaced by LUCK (living under correct knowledge).

CHAPTER 6

Your happiness will be found *through* the choices you make and your ability to *live* in the present.

Ultimately, will striving for excellence, creating strategies, and meeting goals make you happier in your life, professionally and personally?

My experience and belief is that any time you allow yourself to be productive and see the outcome of what you desire, you automatically feel a greater sense of well-being. It simply happens!

GET ACTIVE, STAY ACTIVE

Happiness comes from the successful outcome of a desire … but this can be fleeting if your desires are *not* met. Then you become unhappy.

So, is there any realistic resolution to this dilemma? Contemplate this for a moment:

> *Any time you are focused on the solution*
> *to a situation, you feel better, whether the*
> *challenge is growing a business, dealing*
> *with a health issue, or resolving a conflict.*
> *When you focus on solutions, finding*
> *answers, and not despairing, you remain*
> *in the present and keep your mind from*
> *wandering into the future and activating*
> *the "what if" syndrome.*

Simply put, you must be active. You must move forward. You must pursue excellence in any given situation. This allows your spirit, your inner self, to feel optimistic—and optimism brings hope. Hope and faith, in turn, create within you a greater sense of well-being.

Happiness, in my opinion, is not a temporary state of ecstatic exuberance. Rather, as much as we can experience it, it is a consistent state, a sense of inner well-being. It is knowing that no matter what, everything will work out as it should; having faith in the positive outcome; putting your best effort forward—today, in this present moment, with the cultivated habit of striving for excellence in every situation.

NO ROOM FOR FEAR

Happiness is never acting from despair or depression. Acting from despair or depression is not cultivating the habit of excellence; it is fear. You cannot be outstanding and pursue excellence when you are full of fear.

Looking for solutions empowers us—and when we feel empowered, we automatically feel better about ourselves. We feel happier, even if the situation has not been resolved!

If your sense of inner well-being improves and is stronger, doesn't that increase your overall sense of happiness, regardless of whether the situation has been resolved or not?

Imagine it as a kind of positive domino effect. You control your attitudes and behaviors in any given circumstance, and this contributes directly to your happiness. Your individual happiness is always under your control because it is ultimately determined by how much you have worked on yourself. This knowledge gives you power! You can act on the situations that arise in life before they act on you, and that very real sense of empowerment will make you stronger in every situation.

The Greek translation for the word *happiness* is "eudaimonia," which is translated from various sources as "having a good spirit" or "having a sense of well-being." Having a good spirit and an increased sense of well-being, no matter how small, gives an increased sense of happiness. That's an advantage worth having!

YOUR CHOICE

There are two factors that continually play out in your everyday life; you are in complete control of them, they directly contribute to your sense of well-being, and you should always be mindful of them. They are: 1) the choices you make within your personal culture, and 2) your ability to stay in the present.

A study conducted by two Harvard researchers, Matthew A. Killingsworth and Daniel T. Gilbert, focused on adults ages eighteen to eighty-eight and concluded that people are happier when they are focused on the present and less happy when their minds are continually wandering. (You can learn more about this study by watching Killingsworth's TED talk on YouTube.)

The tendency for the human mind to wander and think about what is not happening is a cognitive achievement that comes with emotional costs, say the researchers in the journal *Science*, adding, "A human mind is a wandering mind, and a wandering mind is an unhappy mind."

That says an awful lot about the importance of focus, does it not? But in today's society with so many distractions—cell phones, e-mail, and text messages, to name a few—we are easily led away from being present, and this affects our sense of well-being.

Being focused allows us to accomplish a lot more. We do not need to answer every phone call or respond to every text or e-mail. They will all be there ten minutes from now.

Try an experiment with yourself. For fifteen minutes—just fifteen minutes—put away your phone, laptop, or tablet and enjoy being present with yourself. Observe your feelings and thoughts; get to know yourself and your surroundings, and do not answer the phone when in company or at dinner with friends. For those fifteen minutes, ignore all beeps, rings, and buzzers as you focus on one task, one conversation.

This can be difficult, because most of us have become conditioned, and it is now a habit, that the moment we hear a beep, buzz, or ring we reach for some gadget. Uninterrupted concentration in today's society is a greatly underestimated source of productivity and sense of well-being, directly contributing to an overall feeling of happiness.

I urge you to try this. You'll be surprised at the results, even from just fifteen short minutes!

Common sense will tell us that when we feel a greater sense of well-being, it is much easier to pursue, manifest, and realize our greatest vision for ourselves and bring our dreams to reality.

Contributing to your well-being are the understanding, acceptance, and allowance that these two concepts—the choices you make within your personal culture and your ability to stay in the present—prepare you to move forward quickly toward your desired outcome.

ACCEPT THE TRUTH

If you can learn to accept what you imagine is real and not doubt that it can be accomplished, and if you can accept the gifts that you have been given and utilize them, you can begin to put into motion the magic, the alchemy that is you. The fact is:

> *You can manifest anything in your imagination that you feel is part of your life purpose, your vision, or your dreams.*

Accepting that you are unique seems simple, and you have heard it many, many times before, but there is a big difference between hearing something and accepting it as truth. It is in the acceptance that you act. It is in the acceptance of a gift that you receive the benefit. For example, if I constantly try to give you something and you refuse to accept it, you cannot even begin to use it, right?

Accept the fact that you are an incredible gift, not just to yourself but to the entire world and to everyone you meet in society, in your professional environment, and in your family! Accept that the contribution you make is absolutely critical to any environment you are in. The individual contribution becomes the collective contribution—but you have to be willing to accept the contribution that you have been called to make.

The collective cannot be formed without individual contributions. If we individuals will understand and accept our unique individual attributes and act upon them, we can contribute them to the collective.

We need individuals in today's society who are willing to stand up and exercise their unique gifts, unwrap them, work with them, establish personal cultures, exercise personal leadership, and move forward with great courage.

This acceptance is very important because it helps you receive intuitive guidance. Learning to listen and accept that inner voice, allowing it space and time to be heard in your life, will give you the guidance, the prompting, the hunch, the sixth sense to move forward with courage, faith, and divine support.

Accept and allow everything to manifest—first internally and then externally, because that is the sequence of events for a truly sustainable outcome.

However, you cannot receive something you're not willing to accept. You must accept it. Your feeling of self-worth is directly tied to your ability to accept, receive, and execute that which you have been given. You should always feel humbly worthy (not egotistical) of the great, unique instrument you own and the contribution you have been given to make through the instruments called the human body and mind.

Develop a conscious awareness of a spiritual, divine inner prompting that moves you to great action with courage, commitment, and conviction to your personal vision and ideal that no one else can define for you. No one else can see what you see, and no one else can make it happen. Only you can do it!

LIVE FREE!

Your acceptance frees you from the status quo. You are a unique individual. You no longer have to live with "what if" thoughts. Reject them, for they are not your reality. Why restrict yourself in a self-imposed prison cell?

I've often wondered why people would, by their own choice, allow themselves to be imprisoned for not doing anything wrong. The "what if" mentality is jail!

So why handcuff and imprison yourself? Freedom to express yourself is your individual divine birthright. It is the key to unlocking yourself from any self-imposed restrictions.

Be mindful of this gift; make sure that it is used correctly, with consideration for yourself and everyone around you. Try to connect with others as you accept your gifts and theirs.

Allow others to flourish around you and empower them to use their gifts as you are using yours. That way everyone benefits from the individual contribution becoming the collective awareness in community, politics, and professional contexts. Only then can we take things to the next level.

Reaching the next level is only possible when we all accept and allow for this paradigm shift to occur. It must happen at every level, and it can if we support each other in the manifestation of our vision for a greater, more sustainable society and professional work environment and a greater connection to each other.

This next level essentially allows us to be connected with ourselves and our true vocations and visions. It is in this interconnection with ourselves and others in true sincerity, not manipulation or ulterior motives, that we can all, collectively and individually, have a greater sense of well-being. That's taking things to the next level!

Whatever you choose to accept is what you will receive. It will be the reflection of your life, because acceptance perpetuates the ongoing choices that you make. That is why acceptance and choice go hand in hand.

If you choose to accept any situation, then your choices will be reflected in that acceptance. Obviously, if you choose not to accept the situation, the automatic requirement will be for change. That change of a situation will bring you a greater sense of well-being, and as discussed before, any time you have a greater sense of well-being, it contributes to your happiness—and, therefore, your ability to accomplish anything increases exponentially.

As you can see, everything is working in concert with everything else. Line up dominoes and knock down the first one; you get an instant domino effect, and that's exactly what we are talking about. All areas of life are connected, which is why having them in sync is so vitally important.

MAKE CORRECTIONS AT THE RIGHT TIME

There is a right time and a right place for everything. It only makes sense, then, that in order to get the results you want, you will need to make corrections at the right time. That also means that it's not necessary to make huge changes in your life all at the same time!

Occasionally you may have to make a lot of changes all at once, but you may be surprised that once you begin to make a small change, everything else around you begins to change as a result. Making small corrections at the right time can give you big results, so don't feel pressured to take on too many changes at once.

Making a correction at the right time is critical. It stops things from breaking loose, getting worse, or completely falling apart!

We all know when something is not right. It may start out small, like a simple toothache, but it can't be ignored. If you ignore it, the pain will only increase and the damage will be many times worse. If, however, you take action right away with some preventative care, the toothache stops its escalation and the correction is successful.

Likewise, proactively (rather than reactively) making small corrections in a timely fashion is going to help you in countless ways, not to mention the fact that it keeps your stress levels down and your health improved.

YOUR ACTUAL STATE VS. YOUR IDEAL STATE

When I work with organizations, I often need to compare their *actual* state versus their *ideal* state. The difference between these states shows where they are now compared to where they want to be.

On a personal level, it's the same thing. You know where you are now with events, situations, and people in your life, as compared to where you ideally would like to be.

This "gap analysis" is also a great place to start the process of goal setting. When you know where you are and where you would like to be, based upon your vision and establishing goals using the SMART concepts, you can begin to close that gap.

Sometimes the gap between the actual and the ideal is quite substantial. The natural question is, "How do we begin to close these gaps?"

My answer, for a company or an individual, is always the same: Begin to work on some of the smaller areas, and automatically the gaps in the large areas begin to close. That is because everything correlates. And when the smaller, easier-to-fix gaps are worked on, that naturally helps the bigger gaps as well.

As you work on your vision and manifesting everything into reality, you will soon become aware of this principle. Sometimes we become so overwhelmed when we look at the gap in front of us. We think it's an insurmountably huge chasm.

It's not really that big. You can overcome it! Take one thought at a time, stay in the present, prioritize and accomplish that one task, celebrate the accomplishment, and then move forward.

Practice this over and over, and the gap will close, your anxiety will decrease, and your goals will become larger because you are closer to accomplishing them.

Be gentle with yourself, love yourself, and remember that Rome was not built in a day!

CHAPTER 7

Cultivate a positive effect in your *own* sphere of influence: your relationships.

Give yourself permission to take some time off to rest; don't allow people or situations to dictate the pace at which you live or work to accomplish something. Allow yourself the ability to be you.

This may sound simple, but it's not. If you don't allow yourself to have your feelings, wants, and needs, and give yourself permission to voice them, they can become constrained without expression. This allowance gives you the ability to meet your own requirements—not at the expense of others, but in the inclusion of others. Unless you can be your best self to yourself, you cannot be your best self to anyone else, and there are certain things that you need to have in order to operate at your best.

Whether you achieve this ideal state simply by spending time alone, taking a hot bath, going for a walk with a loved one, or spending a weekend with your family, it is important to understand that it's okay to admit to your needs. Again, this is not being selfish and it is not at the expense of others.

Interestingly, this acceptance goes both ways as we begin to understand what others need to be their best. If we are meeting each other's needs sincerely and honestly, then we will all be the best we can be.

In relationships, this reciprocation is especially important. It is vital that both people verbalize their sense of vision, what they feel, and how each can help the other. When both parties focus on the needs of the other as well as their own needs, a successful relationship can occur.

On the other hand, if you are in a relationship that is one-sided, where the other person is considering only his or her own needs and you are also considering that person's needs, then who is considering *your* needs? You may as well be alone and take care of yourself!

Some relationships are like that. The fact is, that's really not a relationship at all. It's a one-sided equation that will eventually result in zero compatibility and failure. When two people come together, working in sync with each other, there is alchemy and magic! That is how successful relationships are built.

AIMING FOR A WIN-WIN RELATIONSHIP

Leaders in organizations need to be fully aware of the fact that they are serving the needs of the members of that organization, just as the members of the organization are serving the needs of that company. This is, once again, a reciprocating relationship.

Most companies invest in a vision statement because they want to define the future imagined state of the organization. Individually, we should have our own vision statement as well.

Every organization understands that the vision cannot be accomplished without consistent buy-in from the members of the company. Temporary and sporadic won't do it. Ongoing, innovative partnership is a must if the vision is ever going to come to pass. The members and the vision must be in sync, and this happens when everyone participates with appropriate and pertinent ideas. This process accesses the many creative minds, and it moves the whole organization forward.

All successful people understand this principle in detail. It's important to accept some of the ideas put forward and experiment with them; through allowing innovative partnerships to be established, and accepting some of the ideas and processes presented through these alliances, individuals and organizations become more effective.

Within an organization the leadership form the organizational culture. In a family, the culture is established by the parents—which means that their habits and behaviors influence, for better or worse, everyone else within that family.

On a personal level, you want to manifest into reality your vision and your dreams, right? To do so, your power of influence will have to be extraordinary, positive, and empowering. You are in other circles of influence at work, at home, or with friends, and yet you must exert your own influence. That can be tough.

You must understand the principles, moral compass, character, and credibility that you bring to your world. That is the influence that will touch everyone and everything around you. It isn't just what you say, but what you do, for words and actions go together.

You need to talk the talk and walk the walk!

MAXIMIZE YOUR INFLUENCE

The sum total of your influence, whether it is on your family, professional environment, or social circle, is based predominantly on two very important attributes: your words and your behavior.

You have no doubt heard the phrase, "saying one thing and doing another." It happens all the time. If you do it, you lose credibility. You cannot lead yourself or others if the influence you have is not positive. This simply means that you are not living up to the expectations you have of others.

An illustration of this principle in motion was given by the great Mahatma Gandhi. Gandhi was one of the most influential leaders of the twentieth century. He commanded no great army, had no great wealth, and possessed no title, yet he had tremendous influence. He affected two other major figures in history: Nelson Mandela and Martin Luther King Jr. King visited India in 1959 and referred to Gandhi as "the guiding light of our technique of nonviolent social change." Mandela wrote an entire article about Mahatma Gandhi for *Time* magazine, entitled "The Sacred Warrior."

Albert Einstein said of Gandhi, "Generations to come will scarcely believe that such a one as this walked the earth in flesh and blood."

Gandhi fought for India's independence from the British Empire in the 1900s by applying his own unique vision of freeing India with nonviolent resistance to British rule. His vision was manifested into reality.

What Gandhi said and how he behaved contributed to his great influence, as the following story demonstrates.

> During the 1930s, a young boy had
> become obsessed with eating a lot
> of sugar. His mother was very upset

with this. But no matter how much she scolded him and tried to break his habit, he continued to satisfy his sweet tooth. Being totally frustrated, she decided to take her son to see Mahatma Gandhi who was the boy's idol.

She had to walk many miles across the country, for hours under scorching sun, to finally reach Gandhi's ashram. There, she recounted her difficult journey and shared with Gandhi her unpleasant situation.

"Bapu (Father), my son eats too much sugar. It is not good for his health. Would you please advise him to stop eating it?"

Gandhi listened to the woman carefully, thought for a while and replied, "Please come back after two weeks, and I will talk to your son."

The woman looked confused. But she took the boy by the hand and went home. She made the long journey home and in two weeks' time made the journey once again as Gandhi requested. When they arrived, Gandhi looked directly at the boy and said, "Boy, you should stop eating sugar. It is not good for your health."

The boy nodded and promised he would not continue this habit any longer. The boy's mother was puzzled. She turned to Gandhi and asked, "Bapu (Father), why didn't you tell him that two weeks ago when I brought him here to see you?"

Gandhi smiled and whispered in her ear. "Mother, that time I was not qualified to advise the little one because I too, was same like him, eating a lot of sugar myself two weeks ago."[1]

It was Gandhi who said:

You must first be the change you want to see in this world.

LEADING WITH SINCERITY

People know whether or not they understand and connect with what they are hearing. This is an intuitive

---

1   http://justinhau140.blogspot.com/2010/08%20ghandi-sugar-story.html

sense. It's not something they think about in a logical manner. You've no doubt experienced this as well when you hear something that does not resonate as truth to you. There is no emotional connection. You *hear* it, but you do not *feel* it, and because you don't feel it, it cannot have much influence on you.

This is how it works:

> *What you hear will have a temporary*
> *effect on you, but what you feel and*
> *connect to emotionally will have a*
> *permanent effect upon you.*

For example, if someone tells you that they love you and you *hear* the words but don't *feel* the emotion, it has little effect on you. It may even have a negative effect.

However, if someone says they love you and you not only hear the words but also feel the emotional connection, it has a much more profound, sustainable, and positive effect on you, doesn't it? This is because it comes from their internal genuine love for you. It is sincere.

The power of influence lies in the ability to be sincere, to have genuine care and emotion for another individual. This is why empathy is such a powerful emotion. Empathy is not sympathy. Rather, empathy means that you understand from empirical knowledge. You internally own the experience and feelings of another person and can relate in a deep and compassionate way. It's like you are sharing the experience.

In order to positively and effectively influence any individual, you have to want to share their experience with them. You may not always be able to be empathetic, but you can always be available emotionally and compassionately in the appropriate manner to assist as best you can. This is the power of great personal and professional leadership.

Sympathy, on the other hand, is the ability to feel sorry for someone. You may not have had a similar experience at all, but you feel sorry nonetheless. For example, suppose you meet a woman who lost her father or mother, but you've never had a single death in your family. You can still have sympathy for her, but empathy would emerge if you had lost a parent and were able to understand from your own experience the emotions she was going through. When you can access similar emotions in yourself, you have empathy.

However, do not underestimate sympathy; it has to be as genuine, if not more so, than empathy. Sympathy and empathy demonstrate the extraordinary power and influence you can have on an individual's response to you based on how you respond to them.

You know when someone genuinely cares about you and the ongoing, changing events and circumstances of your life. How you perceive that genuine care influences and determines your behavior toward them.

If you had a bad experience and someone within your family or your work environment was indifferent about it, would that influence the way you thought about that person? Of course. And would that affect what you would be willing to do, or not do, for that individual? Absolutely.

On the opposite side of the spectrum, if you had a bad experience and someone was genuinely empathetic or sympathetic to you, would that influence your feelings about that person and how you might act in the future? For sure!

USING YOUR INFLUENCE

Influence is very subtle; we do not always know our influence on people or situations. It's tough to read every situation correctly.

For example, in a court with a jury, the jury members are no doubt being influenced even if they show no emotion. People do not always show emotion or reveal what they are thinking—so your influence may not always be apparent.

Much of our influence is based on subtle energy exchange through nonverbal, internal, and inadvertent gestures that influence a situation in a second. For example, have you ever witnessed someone in a conversation inadvertently roll their eyes, cuss, gesture, or make an offbeat comment? Maybe it was a job interview or a date or a business meeting; though the person wasn't aware of the action, it made an impact.

The degree of influence might not have been immediately apparent, but the action did not go unnoticed.

That one action, word, or gesture will have a subtle influence on the remainder of the interaction. You may not understand or even be aware of the sudden shift or tone of the interaction, but the perception was influenced by you and your actions, and that influence will affect the outcome.

Has something like that ever happened to you? Everything was going well and yet you couldn't understand the end result. What happened? Maybe you were not aware of the influence you had because it was not overtly apparent. Influence is sometimes unspoken. Sometimes it is apparent only after the event, and it may leave you guessing what went awry.

Your influence manifests itself in many ways. It can be verbal, nonverbal body language, the way you dress, your handshake, your haircut, the way you walk, the apparent state of your health, ethnicity, tone of voice, perceived competence, confidence, and more. Every single influence is subtle, yet it's there.

You cannot control everything. Nobody can. The fact is:

The only influence you can bring to bear
upon any situation is the excellent you
being as outstanding as you can be, having
defined through deep self-analysis and

CHAPTER 8

Find the *freedom* to manifest your
dreams through self-discipline.

F reedom is really the ability to choose the outcome you want. The ability to exercise your freedom, your free will, is an essential part of you. It allows you to choose what you want to do, when and how you want to do it, and whom you want to include.

A part of your free will is your decision-making process. Making decisions and facing their consequences requires a certain amount of self-discipline if you are going to accomplish everything that you have set out to do.

SELF-DISCIPLINE IS GOOD MEDICINE

Just because something feels good and may bring you a temporary moment of pleasure or satisfaction does not mean you automatically have to act upon it and satisfy that desire. Your actions may have consequences that will be detrimental to your personal or professional life. Self-discipline is critically important in the accomplishment of any dream or vision.

Without self-discipline and the understanding of your own innate nature and personality, you can become more destructive than constructive to your overall well-being. Self-discipline contributes to your happiness and thereby your effectiveness.

Understanding yourself and your tendencies, given your own personality, is critically important. Once you understand what easily distracts you and which of your traits tend not to serve you, you can start to address them. Armed with self-discipline and understanding, you can begin to change them. Through self-discipline, you can address your natural tendencies toward needs that you feel are essential, but may not serve you in accomplishing your vision. You like it, but it's not helping!

For example, if you have a natural tendency to be very sociable, but feel it is essential to your well-being and the accomplishment of your vision that you exercise some self-discipline, try cutting some of your conversations short. Be very selective in what and whom you include in your social calendar, and free up more of your time to pursue your goals. Only you can create more time in your day by the choices you make. Be committed to the realization of your vision through your own self-discipline.

We are all given freedom to choose to discipline ourselves. Nobody is given any more or any less time in a day than anyone else. We all have the same amount; it is simply a matter of how we choose to spend our time and what we choose to focus on.

Your free will determines your time, which means that you are in direct control of your destiny. It's not fate, other people, the situation, circumstances, your parents, or your environment. It's you and your free will.

The fact of the matter is:

Anything and everything can be changed
by you at any given moment in time.

The current, present moment you are in will shape your future. Any action you take now will determine the next action that follows, and each accumulated action creates the next.

You know that what you focus on expands. In order to focus on anything, it is absolutely essential that you are self-disciplined. Focus requires self-discipline.

Self-discipline is also vital to the actions and behaviors that correspond to your goals for manifesting your vision into reality. Self-discipline will allow you to enjoy the sense of accomplishment that comes from achieving anything that you set your mind to.

IT'S YOURS IF YOU WANT IT

Setting your mind to do something is only one part of the equation. Your mind cannot accomplish anything without your will. Willpower is directly correlated to self-discipline. You must have the willpower to make the right choices at the right times, and that takes courage, commitment, and conviction to pursue and accomplish what you have set out to do.

There will always be distractions, interruptions, and time lost. Before you know it, the days are gone, the week is gone, and what you set out to do has not been accomplished. It takes willpower, along with self-discipline, to get the job done.

You could say that self-discipline means self-mastery, and self-mastery means freedom. When you have mastered yourself, you are not at the whim of every distraction or temptation. You understand that if something comes along that offers you a fleeting moment of pleasure, it may have a permanent effect on your life! You take it very seriously because you are focused on achieving something worthwhile.

Knowing and controlling the priorities in your life and limiting the distractions (people, cell phones, etc.) will add up to the amount of time available to focus on the accomplishment of your dreams.

Kahlil Gibran says it this way:

> *Your daily life is your temple and your religion. Whenever you enter into it, take with you your all.*

Essentially, most of what I've explained here could be thought of as common sense—but as the saying goes, "The trouble with common sense is that it's not so common."

What is common sense? I like to think of it as wisdom. It is not something that can be learned from a book; it is acquired through deep and constant introspection, learning from past experiences, and taking into account the simple law of cause and effect.

Learning to apply common sense to your life will give you an infinite source of wisdom. You will then always have a solution mind-set to the circumstances in your life. Wisdom is infinite and issues in life are numerous, so seek out wisdom for the solutions you need.

You will find that most of the solutions you seek, to help you with every situation you might face, are already within you. You just need to learn how to get still for a moment, be present, and listen to the inner voice of wisdom that is always waiting to guide you.

I sincerely wish you the best of LUCK (living under correct knowledge) in manifesting your vision!

ABOUT THE AUTHOR

LINTON BERGSEN is a sought-after speaker, author, and champion of change. An inspired communicator and strategist, he has a record of enhancing performance for individuals and companies, including start-ups, privately held businesses, and Fortune 500 industry leaders.

His expertise is in communicating across all levels of an organization, identifying problems, and providing effective solutions. He excels in both one-on-one settings and group seminars, helping people realize their full potential.

Building on the belief that as a leader you can only change an organization if you yourself can change, Linton knows how to get the best out of people and how to identify ways in which people inhibit their own success.

By training the trainer and motivating managers, Linton helps people achieve their full potential. He facilitates organizational development, which leads to improved operations and bottom-line growth. He invests time in understanding an organization's vision, mission, and culture, including its leadership style, and applies that knowledge to interviewing, behavioral hiring, succession planning, and leadership development.

Through the development of an Organizational Needs Inventory, addressing where a company is now and where it would like to be, Linton sets the strategic direction for successful reorganizations. He builds strong teams and coaches on communication techniques to share institutional knowledge, thus creating a common vision and goal.

Enterprising and entrepreneurial, Linton has risen through ranks to inspire and guide leaders, people and organizationsions in diverse industries both domestically and internationally. He has been the president and CEO of his own leadership consulting and personal development company for the past fifteen years.

Linton has a powerful life–changing message, one he shares as a compelling speaker and in this book, *Purposeful Vision*. The message will lead you to the reality of your purpose.